You're Not Alone

You're Not Alone

Holly Deprima

To order additional copies of this book, contact:
Xlibris
844-714-8691
www.Xlibris.com
Orders@Xlibris.com
828172

**Pain changed us, but we can survive.
We can be free.**

Listen Up

Trigger warning! This book contains deep and dark details of situations and feelings. Most of these poems and journals you read in this book are based on real-life situations that others have experienced or felt emotionally. As you read, you will be experiencing what goes on in the minds of those who suffer from mental illness and those who suffered through tough situations. You will also read some stories that relate to me personally, but I will let that remain a mystery. We all have a story to tell. This book is to show you that you are not alone. We all go through hard times and feel things that we don't want to feel. and the world expects us to hold it in and stay silent. Well, I am here to tell you that you don't have to. I am writing in hopes that those who find themselves in dark places will be able to find some type of hope and motivation to keep fighting and make it through and know they are not alone. The only way we lose in life is if we give up. When you find yourself in a dark place, you constantly must remind yourself that this is not a permanent situation. Life will never be perfect no matter how much we try to make it that way. We all have flaws, and there is no such thing as a perfect person. Every relationship, friendship, job, parents, and family has its ups and downs, but we must remain strong and work through them. It is OK to walk away from the people and things we love when it starts to become unhealthy and toxic for your mind, body, and soul. Help yourself before you help the ones around you. Everyone needs to take part in self-care mentally, physically, and emotionally. I learned that setting small goals for yourself is lighter on the shoulders and makes a huge difference when it comes to being overwhelmed. Do not be so hard on yourself. Your only human and we all make mistakes. Do not ever compare your success to others—this is not a competition—and we all need to learn to lift each other up. We all have our own pace, and it is especially important that we do not get discouraged. Being mentally free takes time and dedication and strength. If you do not like your situation, only you can change it. Only you can give yourself what you need. It's a lot easier said than done. Trust me. I know. When you start making yourself a priority and learn to love yourself, everything starts to fall into place. So if you fall, get up and try again. Only you can make a change, and only YOU can make YOU happy.

Contents

Listen Up vii

Chapter 1
The Pain, the Darkness

Journal 1
Thoughts 2
You Don't Like Me Because I'm Me 5
I Die Alone 6
Don't Forget About Me 7
I Could Never Be You 8
I Will Break Through 9
Lift Yourself 10
Justice 11
Journal 12
Hollow 13
Who Am I? 14
Rock Bottom 16
My Demons 18
Just Imagine 20
Free Yourself 21
Depression 22
The Devil in Us 23
Empath 24
I'm Still Standing 25
The Mask He Wears 27

Sweet Sixteen 29

A Pretty Picture.. 30

Afraid of the Truth.. 31

Put It to the Past 32

Heavy.. 33

Stranded Girl 34

Time Alone 36

Monster... 38

Journal 40

Insomnia... 41

A Cry for Help 42

Not My Home 43

I Cry Alone 45

Never Eye to Eye 47

Falling Out 48

Liar 50

At My Last.. 52

Lost It All.. 53

Journal 54

The Problem Child 55

God's Plan 56

Last Party.. 57

Reality of Me 60

Lesson Learned 62

Trust Issues 64

You Slipped Away.. 65

The Other Me.. 66

Withered Heart... 67

It Lingers... 68

RIP 69

Don't Leave Me Here 70

How I See Me 71

Closure...72

Journal..74

Time for Change...75

Beautiful...76

It's OK to Be You..77

Love Is Love...78

Weighing Me Down...79

My Own Battle...80

The Wild Child..81

Post-traumatic Stress..82

Almost to the Finish Line...83

I Can't Be Fixed...84

The Sky Is Dark...85

Let's All Wear the Crown..86

Put Yourself First...87

Love Yourself in the Dark..88

Time Is Ticking..89

Not Who I Used to Be..90

No Destination...91

Chapter 2
The Exhale, the Happiness

Journal..95

My Littles...96

I Never Knew Wishes Would Come True..................97

Heaven's Eyes...98

And Just Like That..99

A Promise Was Made...100

A Book of Us..101

Written in the Sand..102

Overdrive..103

I Walk with Him 104

Found My Way 105

I Won't Look Back 106

Journal 107

Chapter 3
The Voices of Others

A Blessing in a Dark Place...111

Life without a Rose 112

My Journal...114

Flight 115

My Story 116

Survival from Abuse...119

My Baby Was Born 121

Phoenix...122

Unforgiven 124

Chapter 1

THE PAIN, THE DARKNESS

Journal

What's the point of life? I mean, seriously, why are we here and what is the real purpose? How do we stop being a prisoner of our own mind and live happily ever after? Life doesn't make sense to me, and I'm sure everyone can relate. Not everyone was dealt a good hand in this game we call life. Most of us are trying to play the hand we are dealt with the best way we can. Some win, some fail, and some of us are stuck between winning and losing, and that's where life gets difficult, trying to reach the winning goal and struggling not to fail. We have two perspectives in life, and that is looking at life and situations in a positive way or in a negative way. Which one are you? Either way, who am I to judge? I'm playing this life game with you. Some days we think of the worst and hope for the best because we are afraid and tired of being let down. Some of us believe that if you think positively, you can talk great things into existence. Either way, we all deal with life differently, but what we can all agree on is life is one hell of a game. But keep in mind we all have a story and felt pain and happiness. We all know what it feels like to be alone. But the truth is none of us are alone.

Thoughts

I'm not happy anymore. Sometimes I feel like a part of me is missing, like I'm just here standing still while the world continues on around me. I just want to be happy again. I feel empty and alone even though I do have a few in my corner. I don't feel the highs of happiness. Somewhere along the road, I had let myself go, never having the time to be here for myself. Lacking energy and self-motivation, I feel like I'm just not enough. I try to stay strong and to keep a smile on my face, but on the inside, I'm crumbling into small pieces.

I break down when no one is around. Standing still in the shower as the hot water beats down on my skin, I cry.

It's so hard to stay strong. Scared to vent at anyone in fear that your words will be repeated or fear that you will be looked at as weak. I mean let's face it. No one really gives a shit. People have their own problems.

It's draining, constantly overthinking the words people have said to me or being able to read one's actions. People will call you crazy, but in the end, it was all true. Socializing is a back-and-forth thing in my life. Like I want to be around people, but at the same time, I want to be alone. Most days I just don't feel like myself. A lot of times, I find it hard to start my day. You can't even talk about how you feel because the world is cruel and judgmental. People will call you crazy or tell you to just get over it, or they even say that you're overreacting. Oh, and my favorite one of them all is when you try to communicate to people and they take it as an argument when all I'm trying to do is form an understanding. I am so tired, feeling like I'm stuck. I just want to be me again. I am no longer the best version of myself. And please don't judge this book by the cover because I'm fighting these demons in silence. My smiles are no longer genuine. The only thing that keeps me going is my children. I guess, to most people, I'm too much to handle. When you're so used to being strong and surviving through life, it's hard to let someone in. It's hard to let your guard down even with the people you love the most. The words, "I love you," are becoming played out. It doesn't have the same meaning it used to. In this day and age, you don't know who is being genuine anymore. People you've known for years will fuck you over, always pointing fingers at you because they can't handle taking responsibility for their own actions. Too much pride has gotten in the way. Has anyone noticed that when your down and out, everyone says they support you and will be there? Or even congratulate you when you finally get a job, be married, or even when you passed a test? But once you move past them in life, they start to distance themselves. You no longer have their support. These people just disappear. No one helps push each other up anymore. These people were never really there for you. They become jealous and become the snakes in your circle. Small acts of kindness go a long way. I feel like this whole world is in a fighting ring. Everyone separated because of race, religion, sexuality, politics, disability, and so forth. Why can't we all just get along and be happy? Be accepting of everyone. You may not agree with something, but that's not your life to live. So long as they are a good person, that's all that should matter. Don't let how you grew up consume you. I get it. I know things in your past eat at you, and it can creep up on you out of nowhere, but you have to keep looking forward. That's where your strength comes in. You have to eat that shit and use it to your advantage. Let those hard times make you a better person. Be the person you needed to be. Let those who did you wrong show you the person that you should not be. You're not alone. I know many of you that are reading this is thinking, Damn, I can relate to this. I know you may not relate to all of it, but you can feel and understand some things I'm telling you here. Just remember to let go of the ones who don't bring you peace. That's when we can start finding ourselves. Your circle is a reflection of you. Keep the four quarters and get rid of the one hundred pennies. I'm sure you may have heard that saying, but it's true. It means you can have a hundred "friends" who are worth nothing. Or you can have four friends who are worth everything. Your surroundings play a big part of who you are.

Let go and be free. There is nothing wrong with loving yourself. Start here and now. Sometimes we don't know how to love ourselves, and that's something I can't show you how. That's something you have to seek on your own. Until then, do what makes you happy and what's best for you. Life is pretty much a card game. Some of us have a good hand, and some are shitty. It's all about how you play them. Don't beat yourself down anymore. You got this.

—Strength.

You Don't Like Me Because I'm Me

Kill them with kindness,
they are going to hate you regardless,
A world of jealousy. People are heartless.
It's a cold world we live in. Among dark souls,
Stepping on the next person just to get to the gold,
Believing rumors and spreading fake news,
Instead of pulling each other up,
We keep other down and leave them bruised.
You point your fingers at others,
Only because you're afraid to face your own demons,
You judge others and find hateful reasons.
Let go of the pain inside you,
It makes you ugly and weak,
Wash your tongue off hatred before you decide to speak.

–Don't become bitter. Become proud.

I Die Alone

I no longer burn from the pain. My skin turned to ash,
For dust I will be, no more looking back.
No more bones left in my body, completely withered away,
Don't want a funeral. Everyone, just go away.
Dump my ashes onto the devil's grave,
I will rot in hell. I'm no longer the same.
The hate in me is growing like hellfire,
Questioning if the devil's really a liar.
I have seen things I shouldn't and felt the pain that would kill.
If you knew my story, you would understand the hurt I feel.
I had been drugged and beaten, more than once begged for life.
My gears constantly turning hard to sleep at night.
So close to giving up, hoping life takes its course.
I sit here and die alone, no more remorse.

—Wanting to give up is a dark place.

Don't Forget About Me

I jump into the ocean, sinking into the body of darkness,
Water fills my lungs. Never knew my purpose.
No life jacket for me. I wasn't meant to survive,
The ocean's beast has now swallowed me alive.
I slowly sink to the bottom, life I no longer see,
Memories of you constantly hurting me.
If pain were visible, I would be paintedin black and blue,
Left with scars that remind me of you.
My oxygen is depleted. My heart no longer beats,
The ones who genuinely cared, please don't forget about me.

—Memories can haunt you like they happened yesterday.

I Could Never Be You

I needed you here, I wanted to trust you,
Your back toward me, but I still loved you.
Where was the mother I needed? That's right, you never wanted to be.
Always frustrated with my sister and me.
You act as though you never wanted kids,
Well, surprise, mother, we didn't ask for this.
Now you're alone without family to call on,
Or maybe just happy, not wanting us around at all.
Now that we are grown, you washed your hands off us.
Leaving only one person in your life, forgetting the rest of us.
You're the most cold-hearted woman I know,
Was never there when I needed you so.
Now that I'm older and have children of my own,
I couldn't imagine not wanting my children and being alone.
Maybe you expected us to be perfect, most kids can be wild.
Maybe you should have thought this through before having a child.
I could fully expose you for the things you have done,
But I'm more worried about being a mother to my sons.

—You showed me what not to be.

I Will Break Through

The pressure of my mother's weight sitting on top of my stomach
hand over my mouth and nose, I could not breathe,
Feeling all your weight on top of me.
Struggling for air, I would kick and scream,
Not dumb to what you were doing to me.
You would cry to people about how I was a horrible kid,
But never once discussed the things you did.
We never had long talks or any kind of a connection,
A horrible mother you were. You were a lesson.
You letting go of me became my blessing.
Mental and physical abuse,
people like you should never reproduce.
My children are just as wild, but see, you taught me to not give up.
Your dark ways showed me to always love.

—Let the dark path show you to the light.

Lift Yourself

I pretend to be OK,
going about life with a smile on my face,
wiping away my tears, happiness I chase.
No one really gives a damn, or cares about your story,
You have to fight battles alone through the pain and worry.
I keep my head high even when it feels heavy,
Good things will come that are meant for me.
Being alone isn't so bad,
Sometimes it's the best, a private place to be sad.
Feelings are normal, nothing wrong with hurting,
The pain will pass, so stop worrying.
Easier said than done. I get it. I have been here too,
Felt and been through things, I wouldn't
wish my enemies to go through.
Hold on to yourself as ugly as things can be,
The clouds will soon clear, and you will see.

—This is where strength comes in.

Justice

I can see the pain in your eyes. You're no longer the same.
Tears down your cheeks when hearing your son's name.
Nothing will fill the void, a part of you missing.
A hole through your chest, praying and wishing.
You're searching for answers with your heart hanging by a thread,
Your eyes remain heavy, wishing it were you instead.
You have a little hope, wanting justice for the pain that was caused,
Living every day, a part of you missing, a part of you lost.
It's a sick feeling, feels like you swallowed your heart,
Heaviness on your family, you're slowly falling apart.
You bear the pain. You had no choice,
Who took away your son, please raise your voice!
I pray you find justice; I know my words seem little,
The same sad words don't make you feel any better.
You're going through pain that a mother and father should never feel,
Waking up every morning, wishing this wasn't real.
I see a strong mother, a strong family held tight.
In my heart you will find justice, so a part of you can sleep at night.

—Forever he will be here in spirit.

Journal

Have you ever been so lost that you forgot who you are? I have. Feeling like you're stuck in a dark room, flipped upside down, and unable to breathe. Choking on life and strangled by the pain that lies so deep within you. Your whole world is dark, and there is no one to save you. Begging for death because the pain is so intolerable, wondering what you have done wrong to deserve this. Convinced you're unlovable and your self-worth has dissolved into the darkness. Physical pain starts to feel amazing because your heart and mind cannot take it anymore. Starving to feel loved and to see blue skies again. Every day trying to survive while fighting the demons that haunt your mind. Confused about what is real and what is not. Being used over and over again by those who claim they are trying to help, but they are taking everything you have and draining the energy that is left. Everyone who claimed they loved you disappeared and walked away like you never existed. Completely abandoned and depending on the monsters in the outside world to guide you. Drowning in your own prison with daggers in your back. Barely breathing with a faint pulse, but somehow, you manage to stay alive. What do you do next?

—Keep pushing.

Hollow

Mind and body made of glass,
Wishing the pain will quickly pass.
Lost in thoughts, I sit alone,
I'm here in person but far from home.
Once held hostage by deep thoughts,
Left alone and counting my flaws,
what's inside has become hollow,
Depression is here, a hard pill to swallow.
Skipping along, looking for an escape
Left unconscious, do not resuscitate.
Exhaling the cold air, I give my last breath,
Letting go with nothing left.

—Pain changes us.

Who Am I?

I ask myself, Who am I?
Sitting in a dark room, I begin to cry,
I lost myself,
my heart left crippled and dry.
I remain a dark shadow,
an image you can barely see,

sitting beneath this dark cloud,

that seems to follow me.

Stripped of my identity,
smiles are just for show,
Heartache and abandonment,
no more room left to grow.
Who am I?
I question myself each day,
Cannot seem to find the answer,
my words have slipped away.
My life is a puzzle,
something impossible to put together,
So many missing pieces,
it just never gets any better.
The mere thought of death frightens me,
but at the same time, I do not want to live,
My memories are on replay,
I try my hardest to forgive.
I ask myself again . . . Who am I?
This time my eyes burn with tears,
Lost in a cold world,
trying to face my fears.
I live life in confusion,

a blank stare in front of the mirror,
I only see an outline,
it never gets any clearer.
My shadow has faded,
constantly doubting my sanity,
Darkness has clouded my thoughts,
happy is what I pretend to be.
Who am I?
Broken from love and betrayal,
trying to mend my heart,
but I just don't know how.

I hear the ticking of the clock,
still not one answer I can give,
trying to force a smile,
tell me a reason I should live.
Who am I?
I lift my hands up to pray,
afraid he will not have the answer
and will just look the other way.
I kneel to surrender,
Tears start to fill my eyes,
I ask the question anyway . . .
God, who am I?

—Rock bottom hits differently.

15

Rock Bottom

I had given up on life,
I felt so empty inside,
I ran from different homes,
homes that were never mine.
I would never fit in,
constantly feeling broken,
it feels like forever,
since my family and I have spoken.
I've never seen a future,
always hated the way I looked,
running from all my problems,
every chance that I could.
I wanted to get away
as if there was a happy place,
but all I ever found
was a dark and empty space.
For two years I was homeless,
not a place to call home,
surviving day to day,
I felt alone.
Foster care and group homes,
there was never love inside,
felt like I was in a prison,
for years I had cried.
I gave up on everything,
I even gave up on myself,
walking dark roads,
no one there to help.
Begging for change,
unsure of when I will eat,
walking for miles with pain in my feet.
Strangers walking past me,

all looked the other way,
wondering where and when.
I will sleep every day.
Showers were hard to come by,
clothes I had to steal,
at this point in my life,
I didn't know what to feel.
My whole world had crumbled,
I was at my very last,
I was at rock bottom,
being followed by my past.
The nights were getting colder,
trying to do anything for heat,
giving to others,
all that was left of me.
Survival wasn't easy,
had to give up self-respect,
always self-prepared,
for whatever happened next.
Most nights I had felt sick,
my body so tired and drained,
sleeping in abandoned houses,
watching others poison their veins.
This cannot all be over,
somehow, I know I can make it through,
begging for God's help,
Lord, show me what to do.

—Survival.

My Demons

My whole world is collapsing,
not sure of what I feel,
my demons have come to haunt me,
a horror movie that is real.
My heart aches with sorrow,
the physical pain I cannot explain.
Welcome to the hell I live in,
my mind is going insane.
I pick up the knife beside me,
pressing deep cuts into my skin,
the devil breathes for me,
he lives deep within,
sitting here, crying,
I am down on my knees.
I watch the blood pour;
someone come help me, please.
What did I do to deserve this?
Why must I constantly fail?
Wishing for a life that does not exist,
trying to create a fairy tale.
I know happiness is somewhere,
I felt her once before,
or maybe it was make-believe,
and I'm just not dreaming anymore.
I lost all my hope,
my breath is slowly slipping away,
ignoring the voices in my head,
that is telling me it's OK.
I'm staring at the walls,
tears streaming down my cheeks,
hoping above my name,
will soon say, Rest in peace.
I watch my blood flow,

surrounded by puddles on the floor,
screaming on the inside,
I can't take it anymore.
The ones who said they loved me,
just easily walked away,
family had abandoned me,
without any words to say.
The ones I fell in love with,
ripped my heart out my chest,
they burned my body to ashes,
and just moved on to the next.
I feel myself drifting,
the lights are going dim,
staring at these cuts,
that I sliced so deep into my skin.
I'm starting to become faint,
why did life have to be this way?
Writing my goodbye letter,
but who would read what I have to say?
I tried so hard,
I swear I really did,
but I always felt this way even as a kid.
I went from home to home,
no one ever gave me a chance,
they threw me away like trash,
but I tried to put it in God's hands.
Has anyone really loved me?
Do I really know what love is?
I gave away my heart,
and now I ended up like this.
My heartbeat has become silent,
I watch my life pour onto the floor,
I take my last breath,
now pain I feel no more.

—Dark thoughts.

Just Imagine

Have you ever wished that life was just a dream?
Waking up from a nightmare,
and nothing was what it seemed?
I Have.
Reality hits you
the moment you open your eyes,
the headache comes back,
and the pain floods our minds.
Feeling the lack of energy,
hard to get up and start the day,
the feeling of emptiness
never seems to go away.
What is my purpose?
Unsure of what to do next,
constantly failing at life,
trying to do your best.
Living with regrets,
the best choices never made,
small highs of happiness,
turns black and starts to fade.
What if we just woke up
without dark clouds over our heads,
with a rush of happiness
when getting out of bed?
What if it was all a nightmare
And pain had never existed?
Just imagine for once.
Open your hearts and listen.

—We beg for happiness.

Free Yourself

The truth hurts,
reality we must face,
A long look in the mirror
without putting lies in its place.
We run from what hurts us,
instead of looking the demon in its eyes,
we try to twist the truth
to feel better on the inside.
No matter how fast we run,
the truth remains the same.
Look within yourself,
you have no one else to blame.
We put ourselves in a prison,
burying the truth deep inside,
not living reality,
covering them with lies.
It's time to take a step
and face the inner pain,
accept the truth for what is,
or the guilt will remain.
Set yourself free and let the weight become nonexistent.
Admit all your wrongs,
and free yourself from your own prison.

—We need to face the truth.

Depression

Our mind is our enemy,
cursed with self-destruction.
Deteriorating on the inside,
some of us turn to dust.
We chose to leave the world,
sooner than we had planned.
Some take their last breath,
those that could no longer stand.
Consumed by darkness,
battling our minds with how we feel,
drowning in emotions,
unsure of what's real.
Smiling on the outside
to others, we seem simply fine.
Blindfolded by darkness,
we are running out of time.
Our mind is full of poison,
unable to see what others can
with fear of others judgment,
happiness we pretend.
Feeling normal is our drug.
Every day we go and chase,
some of us find it,
and with some, death takes its place.

—My heart goes to those who didn't make it.

The Devil in Us

What if it's not depression?
Or a diagnosis of mental illness?
What if it was the devil
that managed to get inside us?
What if it was him
who used our minds in his control?
Becoming his puppet,
he darkens our soul.
What if it's the devil,
that uses us to hurt one another,
weakening our minds
and creating enemies with each other?
What if it's him that makes us become ill,
preying on the weak,
and controlling the way we feel?
What if he is using us
to play out his dirty deeds,
making us lose faith,
destroying you and me?
What if it's the devil,
and we are looking through his eyes?
What if he is taking over our bodies,
making us believe in his lies?
What if he is the poison
that otherscall mental illness?
How do we rid him of our bodies?
And return from his sickness.

—A wondering mind.

23

Empath

I can feel the emotions of others,
I can see through their lies,
I can feel when one is hurting,
I can understand the reason whythey cry.
I can feel what those are thinking,
extra-sensitive to those who push away,
I see right through others,
when listening to what they have to say.
I absorb others emotions,
as if I'm living their life,
an emotional roller coaster,
making it impossible to sleep at night.
I can sync with others feelings,
always trying to fix one's soul,
easily absorbing the pain,
trying to make them whole.
I can feel when something is off,
without them in front of me,
does this make me an empath?
Living on a high spectrum of empathy.

-Overthinking.

I'm Still Standing

Blessing in life I earned it,
my life I had to reclaim,
erasing the broken past,
unlearning strangers' names.
Healing wounds that were infected,
life had left its scars,
stitching up the cuts and healing a broken heart.
Putting out the fire that raged so deep within,
exhaling all the smoke,
forgive me for my sins.
Drying puddles of tears,
the salt had burned my skin,
eyes once cherry red,
teardrops past my chin.
My fingertips were shriveled,
as if I was soaking in a bath,
from cleaning up life's mess,
and whatever was put in my path.
Hiding scars that remain,
some are self-inflicted,
regaining all my strength,
the depression has been lifted.
My body was left to rot,
somehow, I managed to stay alive,
waking up from life's nightmares,
realizing I survived.
Bruising around my throat,
from his grasp, I could not breathe,
even though all the pain,
I still haven't given up on myself.
I washed off the blood from others,
at one point, I cleaned up my own,

survival at its best,
fighting all alone.
Blisters on my feet,
for miles I couldn't walk,
dehydrated and thirsty,
at times I couldn't talk.
My stomach constantly ached,
nothing to coat the feeling,
emptiness I tasted,
wasn't quite appealing.
My body once felt weak,
dark circles under my eyes,
days without sleep,
impossible to cry.
My toes had become numb,
my body turned to ice,
found myself giving up,
giving up on life.
I could see my own breath,
the sky so dark and heavy,
but even through it all,
God had never left me.
I'm still standing.

-We are warriors.

The Mask He Wears

I had let my guard down. I fell in love with you,
I thought we were picture-perfect,
it was too good to be true.
I sit here in pain. I can't help but cry,
it's time to let go, it's time to say goodbye.
Shattered emotions since I was young,
the wounds still hurt, but I'm starting to become numb.
You were my dreams,
everything I wished for,
I fell in love with a fairy tale that doesn't exist anymore.
You make it clear I wasn't enough,
hope you found what you're looking for,
on me you had given up.
You made me feel free like there was such thing as a happy ending,
but reality kicked in,
I realize you were pretending.
A project you say.
Well, hopefully, I have passed,
I fell in love with a man who was wearing a mask.
I guess this is what happens,
when you put your heart on your sleeve,
I had honestly thought you believed in me.
I thought magic was real,
such thing as true love,
but my time was too little it was never enough.
A thousand pounds lay on my chest,
it's so hard for me to breathe,
I suffered through all the pain,
what have you done to me?
You knew how to make me laugh,
you found ways to make me smile,
but times like this lasted just for a little while.

You made me think I was number one,
but what number was I?
You had broken innocent hearts,
you had made young girls cry.
I fell in love with a mask,
a person who didn't exist,
I'm just another girl that had been added to his list.
A fake profile,
a false identity I must say,
your heart will be broken by someone someday.
And if not so,
you will be wiping the tears from your daughter's eyes,
because a man hurt her,
the way you made these other women cry.
Remember these words,
you will reap what you sow,
karma will find you no matter where you go.
And once she does find you,
I hope you believe that she cares,
because it's your turn to fall for the mask that she wears.

—Those who hurt us are lessons.

Sweet Sixteen

The phone did not ring on Christmas,
Thanksgiving, or Valentine's Day,
hoping to hear from her on my sixteenth birthday.
But, of course, the call never came.
I knew this was a chance to happen,
but on this important day,
she didn't relay a message, call me, or nothing.
I was hoping that she would,
but my hopes have let me down.
I knew this was a chance to happen,
no reason for my frown.
I thought being sixteen was special,
or was it I who thought that way,
and to her,
it was just an ordinary sixteenth birthday?

—We all need our mother.

A Pretty Picture

My life is like a picture, erase it all away,
use a pretty color to draw a better day.
Draw a happy family,
I will use it for show and tell,
draw a beautiful background
instead of my living Hell.
Put smiles upon our faces,
draw sunshine instead of rain,
draw a happy family,
take away all the pain.
Draw a house in the background,
a family dog by my side,
make me look happy,
instead of the tears I try to hide.
Hang us on the wall,
for everyone to see,
showing off a portrait,
on how I wish life could be.

—Family is important.

Afraid of the Truth

I'm scared to be in love,
afraid of hurting again,
scared to feel special,
afraid it will end.
I'm scared that you could love me,
afraid that you will leave me.
Afraid you will turn away,
afraid you will never think of me.
Scared your feelings are not as strong,
afraid of the possibility,
of you treating me wrong.
Scared to hold you close,
afraid of what you might say,
scared of letting go,
afraid of you walking away.
Scared to tell you how I feel,
afraid of not knowing what is real.
Scared to tell you what's hidden inside,
afraid to show the feelings I tend to hide.

—Life is about taking chances.

Put It to the Past

What kind of person are you?
Why walk away?
Why hurt me deeply almost every day?
Why put me through pain
when all this could stop?
Why do you say you hate me
when I had loved you a lot?
Why do the things you do?
It was always me you try to hurt.
Why didn't you want me around?
Hurting me even more.
I never stopped loving you,
so why did you stop loving me?
Just tell me the truth.
I know you never wanted me.

—We can all relate.

Heavy

When life seems heavy, what do you do?
Living in a world of judgment,
no one to talk to.
Trying to keep your head high,
no one to wipe your tears,
covering the pain with a smile,
pain that's been hidden for years.
I feel the weight of the world.
It's so heavy, I'm about to break,
feeling torn on the inside,
not much more I can take.
Overwhelmed by life and what it put in my path,
draining all my energy,
and taking all I have.
It feels like I am drowning,
little room for me to breathe,
when will life lighten the load that lies so heavy on top of me?

—Just breathe.

Stranded Girl

She was just a young girl,
not even the age of five,
too young to understand death,
left stranded but still survived.
Her stomach growled in hunger,
went days without a bath.
She cried herself to sleep,
her teddy was all she had.
She heard screaming in the next room.
Mommy's boyfriend not so nice,
angry like the devil,
his heart was cold as ice.
Peeking through the cracked doors,
watching Mommy dragged by her hair,
screaming bloody murder as he tied her to the chair.
The little girl hid in the closet,
next to dirty needles on the floor.
All she had seen were a filthy mattress
when peeping out the closet door.
Mommy's screams had become faint,
with the poison they injected within themselves,
heroin and bent spoons scattered on the ground.
Both bodies became limp,
eyes rolled back on their heads,
creeping out the closet,
wondering if it was over yet.
Tears have stained her cheeks,
as she held her teddy to her chest,
looking for Mommy, hoping he had left.
Mommy was still limp,
not once had she moved,
boyfriend was nowhere to be found,

not sure of what to do.
She whispers to her Mommy,
begging her to wake up,
her eyes never opened,
her body never budged.
She yelled to Mommy louder,
tugging on her shirt,
the needle hanging from her arm,
Mommy, are you hurt?
No signs of her Mommy breathing,
the little one's eyes filled with tears,
drowning from the pain,
facing her worst fears.
Mommy's last breath was gone,
no one to call for help,
witnessed her mother's death,
lost in the pain she had felt.
She didn't understand,
sneaking out of the apartment, down the steps,
out the front door, the little girl had left.
A big world outside,
looking for help from a stranger,
telling an older man,
that her mommy was in danger.
The paramedics had come,
mommy covered with a sheet,
her face completely covered,
zippered from head to feet.
The little girl was lost,
suffering from what life had handed,
alone she was,
a young girl that was stranded.

—Everyone has a story.

35

Time Alone

I don't mean to be so distant.
Sometimes I need to be alone.
My emotions have me occupied,
sorry, I can't get to the phone.
Just leave me a message,
I will eventually call you back.
Please, don't give up on me,
I swear you're all I have.
Sometimes I get busy
with the chaos that stirs inside my head.
I need some time for me,
let me crawl into my bed.
I'm sorry it's been a few weeks,
this time it's taking a little longer.
I promise I don't hate you,
I just need time to get stronger.
Please, don't take it personal.
I know I may be acting weird,
but promise you won't leave,
you just can't see me here.
I'm sorry I can't be there
as the friend I claim to be,
trying to keep control of the madness that's killing me.
I promise we will soon catch up.
Right now, I'm a little boring.
Maybe I will feel better,
I'll try again in the morning.
I don't expect you to understand,
I know this may seem quite odd,
but over time, I get this way,
it's hard to make it stop.
These feelings come in waves,

like a dark cloud inside my head.
I wish I weren't like this. I'd rather smile instead.
Sometimes I need my space,
like a scared dog they tend to bite,
backed in a corner, afraid that I just might.
I constantly need reassurance.
Sometimes it feels good just to hear,
Please don't walk away,
that's always my biggest fear.
Just know that I love you.
Right now, I need you most,
at the same time, I need my space,
please come hold me close.

—Depression, that shit fucking hurts.

Monster

I want to walk away,
but at the same time, I don't want to leave.
Nowhere else to go,
you have a hold on to me.
No family for me to call,
true friends I never had,
no one in my corner when life got so bad.
He reminded me I was alone,
that no one would love me as he did,
bruises on my body,
blood drawn from every hit.
He would tell me we were just alike,
sharing a similar past,
being cared for by a monster,
choking in his grasp.
Constantly being blamed
for things I've never done,
trying to avoid arguments,
nowhere for me to run.
A gun pointed at my face,
he breathes heavily with his stare,
blocking the bedroom door,
he pulls me by my hair.
"I f******g love you," he said,
I thought this was it,
squinting from the pain, I felt with every hit.
I tried to calm him down,
telling him what he wanted to hear.
He ripped off all my clothes with his gun sitting near.
I wonder if it was loaded,
attempted to grab and pull the trigger,
I was too scared,

shaking and trembling fingers.
His hands wrapped around my throat,
I could barely breathe,
feeling the weight with him on top of me.
I make it to the bathroom, locking myself inside,
cleaning up all the blood,
eyes filled with tears.
I start to cry.
Every day he says he is sorry,
believing his own lies,
praying I get away and wipe the tears from my eyes.

—Sometimes running away is OK.

Journal

This is it. I don't have a purpose. I was brought into this world to suffer, to constantly feel like I am nothing—unwanted and left alone to rot. I was brought here to be laughed at and used as a stepping stone. It's a cold world out here. All the things you were taught when you were younger were all lies. People are filled with hatred and selfishness. People feel good about the pain they inflict on others. We are made to believe that life is a Disney movie or a fairy tale, but it's not. The world is cold and heartless, and if you get lost out here, you will rot and become part of what's around you. Imagine having absolutely nothing. Imagine having no one. Imagine feeling so alone that you walk through the darkest places, hoping something takes you out of your misery. Imagine everything you ever had was just gone. The people you trusted the most, who claimed they loved you so much just walked away. I was treated like trash and thrown away and recycled repeatedly. I can't even count with all my fingers how many places I had lived or how many times I had to try again and trust that the next person won't get rid of me too. I never fit into anyone's perfect picture. I am just here, being tossed around like I'm less than a human being. Do you have any idea what this does to a person? All I have is myself.

—Poetry has its own language.

Insomnia

Sleep had run away,
constantly in search of her,
nowhere to be found. Deep thoughts occur.
Racing thoughts,
impossible to unwind,
overthinking and going back in time.
Situations on replay,
can't get this out of my head,
pondering on what I should have done instead.
Is there something I missed?
Maybe something I forgot to do.
Sleep, come back right now,
I need you.
Constantly overthinking,
replaying memories from the past.
Tell me this isn't permanent,
and this too shall pass.
Staring in the mirror,
a zombie stares back,
dark circles under my eyes.
My thoughts turn black.
I close my eyes, but everything is numb,
searching for sleep,
but where did she run?

—I'm exhausted.

A Cry for Help

You hear people say, "I'm here if you need me."
But are they really?
Same repeated words when they care less about how you're feeling.
Tell someone you're depressed,
and watch them tell the world you need attention,
cold-hearted at its best,
a world without affection.
The same people will stand at your funeral
as if they had ever cared.
Where were you when I needed you?
Now I'm no longer here.
Remember, I just needed attention.
Now you sit at my side and cry.
I needed someone here.
I didn't really want to die.
But because I felt alone,
afraid you would judge me again,
I buried my feelings deep inside
until it killed me in the end.
Now you sit here, feeling sorry,
wishing this would never be.
Maybe things would have been different,
but you chose to just laugh at me.
"Just get over it."
Your encouraging phrase,
your uplifting judgment,
you made it clear in my darkest days.
You said you were here for me,
but where are you now?
Standing above my breathless body,
six feet underground.

—Be the person you need.

Not My Home

Feels like I'm serving a life sentence,
double-locked behind these doors,
looking out of thick glass windows,
and sleeping in a bed that isn't yours.
It felt like a prison for years,
feeling unwanted. I was thrown away,
locked behind these cylinder walls,
everyone gone so far away.
This place was called the unit,
eight to ten rooms for each floor.
Looking for a way to escape,
I don't want to be here anymore.
Locked away with other children,
some had adapted well.
For me, I didn't belong here,
trying to find a way out.
The doors would stay locked and the windows
bolted shut and would never open.
This is what I call hell,
a prison for children.
Escorted downstairs for school,
my shoes they had taken away,
with only socks on my feet,
I would still try and run away.
This wasn't juvie hall,
but a place for children with "emotional distress."
I called this place a prison,
A psych ward at its best.
Took forever for a placement,
the state was unsure of where I would go,
group homes and foster care,
people I didn't know.

Running away was my new freedom.
One time, I've seen my own missing picture on the wall,
"If anyone has seen her, the police you should call."
Throughout my whole life,
I have moved over a million times,
but none felt like home,
a home that could be mine.

—Where is home?

I Cry Alone

How would you describe her?
I say, cold-hearted and empty,
"She had her 'good child.'
She didn't want me."
The words I hate, you repeated in my head,
crying at night before going to bed.
She made me feel like I was different.
I hated going home.
I getmore comfort from friends,
with her, I felt alone.
I can't count on one hand the good memories we had.
I felt more at home when I was home with my dad.
He never told me he hated me or made me feel like I was nothing.
I was daddy's girl; I was his everything.
Sometimes life happens.
Wishing they would have stayed together.
Would life be different?
Would she have treated me better?
She made me out as a monster,
a child she would give away.
Always wanting her attention,
but she had nothing to say.
I don't even remember a day that I once made her proud,
constantly cursing my name and putting me down.
She was motherly to my sister,
loving her in my face. Made me feel like nothing,
I felt out of place.
Her stare was very cold, never easy to read,
I was what you called "different." She hated me.

I never understood her, and I still don't until this day,
how she hated me so much in every way.
When I look at my children and think about how she had treated me,
she taught me she was the mother I never wanted to be.

—I will never be her.

B

Never Eye to Eye

Be a better parent so they aren't looking for family in friends.
Learn to be a better you so they won't hurt in the end.
I learned to love differently,
to be the person I needed.
It felt lonely growing up and constantly hated.
Going to my mother for advice or help
was a closed door to my face,
a closed book on a shelf.
I tried to be honest and open,
but she would pick me apart
each time I had spoken.
She had created this wall,
a door locked without a key,
unable to talk to her with open honesty.
My secrets left with my father,
with her I refuse to share.
My father kept them for me, she never even cared.
With my father I could be myself,
around him, I was free.
Every other weekend, his time was spent with me.
She never wanted to be bothered,
just wanted us to shut up and behave.
I thank her for teaching me to not raise my kids this way.

—I'll be the mother I needed to be.

Falling Out

My love for you had grown colder,
as you screamed you hated me to my face,
defending myself from your hateful ways.
Every day you would want to argue,
you couldn't keep your hands to yourself,
locking me in the bathroom for hours, it felt.
You would push me around the house,
provoking me to react,
when I finally did, you took advantage of that.
You would tell people I was out of control,
but it was you that pushed me to defend
as if you wanted me to react so you could run to family and friends.
It was as if I was your punching bag.
You would take things out on me,
you were miserable for years, you wanted to get rid of me.
Your title as my mother slowly withered away,
instead, you played the role of a monster every day.
You would tell doctors I was out of control,
and claimed they told you to restrain me,
I ended up fighting you back,
but could you blame me?
Your weight on my stomach,
your hand over my nose and mouth,
is that really the way they told you how?
I couldn't even breathe,
you would stare me in my face,
trying to escape from your tight grip,
your "restraints."
Kicking my feet,
shaking my head side to side,
trying to breathe, you watched me cry.
You dragged me by the hair,

my head hitting the side walls.
Too young to think of suicide,
I wanted to end it all.
I tried so hard to fight back,
you lay bruises on my chest,
sick of your torment,
red marks around my neck.
I would throw things down in your path,
to slow you down to get away,
locked myself in the bathroom for hours until it was OK.
You would smash food in my face and push me out of my chair,
my head would be sore when you ripped out my hair.
Of course, I reacted, started cursing your name,
I wanted things to be better but never looked at you the same.
Any little excuse to put your hands on me,
so I started to run away.
Finally, peace of mind after getting away.
Defending myself,
hitting you back at the age of twelve,
put on probation for defending myself.
Taken to a group shelter home with other girls who were charged,
had community service, she only visited once.
We were taken to a jail, scared straight to Patuxent,
never learned lessons, still constantly running.
I didn't want to go home,
at the same time, I never wanted to stay,
just want to wake up with all the troubles gone away.

—Don't lose yourself.

Liar

You left me in a hot car for hours,
embarrassed for my braided hair,
told me I looked "Black."
But why would you even care?
On our way to a church party,
you told me to stay inside,
in the middle of summer,
for you to enjoy family time.
I sat inside the car for hours.
I know your husband played a part,
A man who always controlled you,
a man without a heart.
You broke me down to nothing;
you would always shame me about my weight.
Later, down the road, my own image I started to hate.
You constantly called me fat or compared me to other girls,
belittled me as nothing,
you didn't care how much it hurt.
I always felt like my mother hated me,
but you always made it worse.
You talk bad about my parents,
trying to make me choose you first.
You told me my mother would always get rid of me on days I was sick,
I wonder if this is true
or did you lie about all of it?
You would take situations and twist the stories around,
you lied to me constantly, putting my family down.
Your husband would be controlling,
cheated on you with his ex-wife,
running back to him like everything was alright.

You would pretend to always "save" me or claim to be proud,
but when I would take a step further,
you purposely knocked me down.
You wanted to see me fail, just to make a story out of me,
my turn to expose you from the person you pretended to be.

—Learn to let go.

At My Last

CPS wouldn't move forward by coming back to live in your home.
After a weekend visit, you left me in a hot car all alone.
I remember you once told me,
you hope I had this life-changing condition,
you said I would get state help,
a place for me and my son to live in.
Who wishes bad health on family?
And why was this even a thought in your head?
Kicking me in and out of your life,
playing a game of pretend.
Your judgement of race was awful,
judging people by their skin,
using my mixed son as a crutch,
a topic to let you in.
Your husband was once a hunter
with a buffalo hanging on the wall,
deer heads, and others, I can't sit and name them all.
He names the buffalo, Buster,
starts calling my son that too,
claimed my child had nappy hair just like the buffalos do.
I had nowhere else to go,
caring for my baby with nothing left,
your husband smiling ear to ear, sticking out his chest.
In the end, I was given an option,
either my son goes or we both leave.
I packed up both our bags.
You will never hear from him or me.
How could she allow him to do this?
Had the nerve to pretend she cared
as she drove me back to the city unsure of what to do next. I was scared.

—I lost everything.

Lost It All

Life had hit me hard.
That's it. I have nothing left,
Unsure of what to do or where we were going next.
I had no other options,
didn't have friends or family for me to call.
I even lost myself. I completely lost it all.
I thought I've done the right thing.
Maybe his father cancare for him just for now,
nothing permanent. I just need to figure it out.
He took advantage of my situation,
kept me from my child for months on end,
gained custody from the courts, the most hurt I have ever been.
Thrown on child support and laughed in my face,
I Granted sole physical custody, visitations took place.
Wasn't given enough time to land on my feet.
He smiled in my face and did this to me.
Using my son for a woman,
telling sad stories of a single father.
Woman suckered in,
He was the biggest liar.
That day changed me,
I fought for six years,
judged laughed in my face
after he would take my son and disappear.
Made me out as a bad mother.
I was homeless for some time.
There was no other issue so explain to me why.

—My heart ripped to pieces.

Journal

Eventually, you get numb to the pain and lose yourself. Feeling that the bad is always outweighing the good and nothing seems right anymore. Through survival, our brain is permanently programmed to overthink. We think of the worst and hope for the best and become negative to ourselves. Self-hate is a strong hellfire that burnt in our brain whenever we look in the mirror. We lose ourselves to the point that it feels like there is no return. Trying to free yourself from those shackles that have kept you down for so long feels impossible, so we stay stuck and try to make good out of the bad and settle with our situations. We feel like we have been cursed and constantly asking ourselves what we have done wrong. People will give us advice, but we blow them off, thinking to ourselves that they have no clue because they have never walked a mile in our situation. I never asked for this, and I do not want to hurt anymore.

—It's time to find yourself.

The Problem Child

I was the problem child,
you know, the kid that couldn't pay attention,
fighting all the time and given suspensions.
In no way was I an angel,
a little devil at its best,
hard to sit still and learn like the rest.
It was hard to stay focused,
to sit still and understand,
following trouble every chance that I can.
Outbursts with smart remarks,
trying to make friends laugh,
expelled from most schools, and ditching class.
I didn't know who I was or what I wanted to be.
I never backed down when someone picked with me.
If the tables had turned and I was the one teaching,
these kids you call "trouble" would be my reason.
The kids following the right path,
most don't need saving.
It's the child you call trouble that needs life teaching.
Get closer to the ones that disrupt your class.
This child is your challenge,
now follow your path.
Most teachers will favor the most well-behaved,
but maybe it's the "troubled" that needs to be saved.

—Make a difference.

God's Plan

Have you ever cried so hard?
Asking God why this is happening to me.
No longer having faith and feeling pain endlessly.
Feeling like the world is out to hurt you with broken
promises and fake love. Begging God for help,
what have I done?
Are we already in Hell?
Was there a past life and I have done wrong?
Repeating mistakes, impossible to stay strong.
I questioned God's love,
even questioned if he was real,
begging him to rid the pain that I feel.
Trying to do the right thing and asking him for guidance,
but in return,
he has given me his silence.
I was at rock bottom, begging for him to take me home.
I didn't want to see tomorrow.
I felt alone.
I wanted to fall asleep and never again wake up.
Life was heavy. I had enough.
If you were in my shoes, do you think you could still stand?
Walking on Hellfire,
was this God's plan?

—Why is this happening?

Last Party

I was taught not to drink and drive,
but I thought one drink wouldn't hurt,
heading to a party with my hair curled in my miniskirt.
My makeup was done perfectly,
feeling beautiful, at its best,
arriving at a friend's party and showing off my dress.
I met up with my three friends,
the only ones from the party I knew,
every song the DJ would play, we were dancing to.
Strobe lights dressed the room
while music filled the air,
a refill on my cup, I start to let down my hair.
I was smiling from ear to ear,
when this cute guy waved from across the room,
walking over with his drink to talk to me, I assume.
He asked if he could join with his eyes locked into mine,
dancing to every song, forgetting about the time.
He went off to grab us drinks after seeing my cup was empty,
I told him only one more and that I was starting to feel tipsy.
My favorite song started to play as we laughed and continued to dance.
I felt like I was free, raising the cups that were in our hands.
Moments later, I felt the room slightly spin.
He grabbed me by my waist and gently pulled me in.
His kiss made me breathless. I didn't want this night to end,
I told him it's been a while. I haven't seen my friends.
He reassured me they were fine, that maybe they went home.
I found it quite odd that they would leave me here alone.
I didn't think twice as he handed me another drink.
At this point, I was wasted. It was impossible for me to think.
With the music still playing, he asked if I wanted to get away.
Still sipping my drink, I agreed and said OK.
I asked where we were going as he led me to another room.

I told him it was getting late, that I had to head home soon.
I told my parents I wouldn't drink and drive,
figured I could use this time to sober up,
but as time went on, I could barely stand up.
My legs started to feel heavy,
my arms would barely move.
It felt like I weighed a thousand pounds,
lying down in a dark room.
I told him I felt weird,
slurring words, I could barely speak.
He told me it was OK as he started caressing me.
He whispered in my ear and told me to just relax.
It was only moments later that everything turned black.
I remember waking up with my skirt above my waist,
stumbling as I stand, pushing my hair out my face.
My underwear was on the floor, saturated with blood,
fighting to keep my balance and trying to pick them up.
I managed to turn the light on,
but he was nowhere to be found,
I don't even remember his name,
still hearing music in the background.
I couldn't have been here long,
I could still hear the DJ play,
straightening my dress in a hurry to leave and get away.
I didn't want to call the police,
afraid people would point and judge.
It was my choice to follow him,
but I don't remember much.
I make my way to the front door,
I stumble down the steps,
I took one last look, but I didn't see my friends.
I managed to get inside my car,
starting the engine, I could barely see,
tears flooded my eyes.
What the hell happened to me?
Barely able to stay awake,

I started to head back home,
that's when a driver ran a stop sign from being on the phone.
She crashed into my car,
my head slammed against the glass,
blood gushing down my face,
everything happened so fast.
I couldn't even move, finding it harder to breathe.
Hearing the sirens, I knew this was the end of me.
Responders pulled me out of the car,
announcing that the driver was dead,
I thought they were talking about them,
but they were talking about me instead.

—Please be safe.

Reality of Me

Numb to the pain that has destroyed me.
I'm a stranger to myself.
Confused as to who I am,
I no longer ask for help.
What's left of me is nothing.
Just empty and out of tune.
I had begged for help.
But for me, there was no room.
I was completely broken down,
walking city streets alone,
no one to talk to
and no one to pick up the phone.
I felt like I was a waste of air
that made those around me suffocate.
I was the burden.
It's me I really hate.
My childhood dreams no longer mattered,
it's now survival at its best.
My life was upside down,
my whole world was a mess.
What if I didn't run away and stayed in those homes that felt empty?
Would my life be any different around those who didn't love me?
These places felt like a prison,
unsure where you're going next.
Five minutes to pack your clothes in trash bags,
barely time to get dressed.
I just wanted to get away and try to make a life of my own
in hopes that life would be better and have a place to call home.
I was never looking back no matter what I was about to face.

I would rather have been dead before I went back to that place.
No one teaches you survival.
You force yourself to make it work.
You suck up the pain and go no matter how much it hurts.

—Life is never easy.

Lesson Learned

Hey, is everything OK?
I was asked by a stranger when walking alone one day.
I said everything was fine in hopes he would leave me be.
He was very persistent as he walked up to me.
He said it was cold outside, for me to take his jacket,
I was wearing short sleeves in October.
He told me I could have it.
"Where are you going?" he said.
It's cold and it's late,
but I wasn't sure myself.
I was homeless and afraid.
I wanted to be somewhere warm.
It's been 3 days since I ate and showered,
walking the streets alone and counting the hours.
He walked with me for a while as if he were genuinely concerned,
but little did I know,
tonight would be a lesson learned.
He talked me into staying at his house
for a night to shower and eat.
I learned the hard way
that the simple things in life weren't for free.
I wasn't familiar with the neighborhood
or had an idea of where I was at,
but this is the end of the story
because this is where everything went black.
I remember waking up
to what seemed like more than one voice in the room.
My arms and legs weighed a ton.
I could not move.
I couldn't see a thing everything was pitch black,
I barely remember anything,
I must have passed out.

I woke up for the second time
in an empty flooded basement.
What did I have to drink? Did he lace it?
The door to the outside was open, no one was around,
I heard fighting from upstairs, I hurried to get out.
I was stripped of my clothes, hurrying to put them on,
crying on the inside,
What have I done?
I left out of the house, unsure of what to do.
I never called the police, afraid of those judging me
I felt like it was my fault,
that I know better to make these decisions,
so why cry for help?
It was my fault, so nobody will listen.
I kept this secret to myself
as if everything was deserved.
I continued as if nothing happened.
This was my lesson learned.

—It's not your fault.

Trust Issues

Unintentionally overthinking
unsure of what is true.
When something does not seem right
my thoughts run wild until they do.
My mind starts to pace.
I scramble for an answer.
Rearranging thoughts like a puzzle
and still unsure about the morning after.
Your response is unbelievable,
my brain wants to make it right.
Pondering on the situation
that has been keeping me up all night.
Overanalyzing your tone,
your body language says different.
Watching your every move
and asking you the same question.
Always feeling like you're being lied to.
I cannot seem to take one's word.
This is the damage from constantly being hurt.

—It can be hard to trust again.

You Slipped Away

I had watched you stop loving me.
You slowly slipped away.
Each day you were different,
you felt so far away.
It felt like my heart had sunken,
a sick feeling in my stomach.
I would ask you what was wrong,
but you would tell me it was nothing.
I would always ask if you loved me,
just so I could hear you say it.
But I was never convinced,
it seemed like you faked it.
You made me think I was overthinking,
that I was crazy to ask that question.
Each day you were farther away,
and with my heart, I had listened.
Now here we are as strangers,
no longer familiar with who weare,
Our time had stopped ticking.
You left a painful scar.
You had stopped loving me
when each day I had loved you more.
My heart crumbles to pieces,
reading your goodbye letter on the door.
Deep down I know it's over.
I just don't want to believe this is true.
Giving the ones we love excuses,
for the things that they do.
Sometimes it's just over.
You were the only one in love.
Heartbroken like your mourning,
after losing him to someone else.

—Betrayal hurts.

The Other Me

The monster inside me has come out to play,
I try to bury him inside, but he tends to find a way.
He has taken over my mind. This is not the person I am.
Addicted to this high, when will this all end?
I have tried to stop, but it's what numbs the pain,
It gives me power; it clears my brain.
I feel stronger than ever, a moment without fear,
but when it's all over, no one is here.
I ended up losing friends, and my family turned their heads.
I want to be normal, but the high takes over instead.
I find myself eating less, my body skin and bones.
I lost everything I had, even my home.
The high I have been chasing makes reality hard to see.
I am no longer able to escape the monster in me.

—There is a way out.

Withered Heart

I have built a wall around me,
so please do not come too close.
I refuse to hurt again,
doing my best to protect us both.
I have withdrawn from connections,
my heart cannot take the pain.
It is time to disappear,
and shelter from this rain.
I no longer look for love,
for it had me facing close to death.
I no longer care for anyone,
for me, I will do what is best.
Remaining sheltered in my thoughts,
my secrets stay with me.
I have blindfolded my heart,
now I can finally see.
I have built this wall with tears,
with every bit of strength that I had left.
I will walk this path in darkness.
I wish we never met.

—Protect your heart.

It Lingers

I don't feel like myself today,
I'm not sure what I'm feeling,
I'm in the need of clarity,
Most of all mental healing.
I need to feel uplifted,
I feel an ache of deep sorrow,
Lingering through the day,
Wishing for a better tomorrow,
What is it to be normal,
To feel whole within yourself?
How do you break this habit?
Inside we cry and call for help.

—Find someone you trust and talk to.

RIP

I wish you never went to that hotel that day.
Now you're gone and so far, away.
A gunshot to your head; he had left you to die.
Now we sit here asking why.
Addicted to hookups and unfamiliar faces,
looking for love in all the wrong places.
You met him online, but you had no clue.
People do it all the time,
but it happened to you.
He had taken your life and left you to bleed.
Now we bow our heads. RIP.

—Here today and gone tomorrow.

Don't Leave Me Here

Don't leave me in this dark place; it's lonely here.
Feelings of emptiness, I'm blindfolded and confused.
Feeling numb on the inside, I really need you.
I'm living in a dark space, waiting for the sun to shine,
Can't explain how I feel when you ask me why.
A sick feeling in my stomach I can't seem to shake,
I need you more than ever, just do whatever it takes.
The feeling of being invisible, trying to fill my empty glass,
sinking deeper in the mud with thoughts of my past.
I want to erase the memories. I no longer want to be scarred.
I know you're sitting beside me, but I drifted too far.
Reaching out for your hand, but I can't get close enough.
An emotional current has drifted us apart.
I need you to come find me. Please don't leave me here,
slowly slipping away and chased by fear.

—Hold on to the one you love.

How I See Me

When I look in the mirror, I don't see what you see.
I feel disgusting, a monster staring back at me.
You call me beautiful, but I feel otherwise,
Doing my makeup, I start to cry.
My hair is never perfect, my clothes don't fit me right,
unhappy with my body, extremely self-conscious.
I see photos of myself on Facebook Memories,
I was a lot smaller; even then, I hated myself
Looking at old photos, oh, how I wish I could go back.
I had let myself go. I drifted miles off track.
I need motivation, only I can push myself,
But first things first, work on me mental health.

—Change starts with you.

Closure

When I ask you, you tell me nothing is wrong.
I watched us grow apart, but my love still lived strong.
You became distant,
as I begged for the love that has been fading before my eyes.
I never stopped loving you,
meanwhile, I was crying on the inside.
Every day you would change.
I tried to change myself to fit your perfect picture.
Your hand that was once in mine,
now has withered.
I'm exhausted,
fighting for the attention you once gave me,
wanting to feel secure like when you use to love me.
I threaten to leave, making it my last resort.
I never wanted to leave; my heart is torn apart.
I tell you I will leave in the hope you will chase me,
wanting a reaction that gives me hope that you still love me.
Actions speak louder than words,
but your silence was all I heard.
If I could rewind time
and fix what made us go downhill,
I'm still uncertain about what to change
because I always loved you;
it was real.
You smile around the ones you love,
but with me, your face turns blank.
My mind starts to race,
and I start to overthink.
I stare at the mirror, hating my body,
wondering what I could do to change.
Dressed up with my makeup on,
but you still come off so strange.

I started to get mad,
feeling like I was being ignored,
Talking to you became like talking to a closed door.
Getting you to pour your heart is like pulling teeth;
maybe it's over, and you fell out of love with me.
Maybe I'm fighting for something that died a long time ago,
and I'm the one still in love, and I just can't let it go.
Facing the truth that what we have is over,
I just needed to hear you say it. I'm in need of closure.

—It hurts.

Journal

I know what it's like to feel nothing. You're watching life fall apart, but you feel nothing, and you no longer care about what's happening around you. At this moment, you become mute, and you find yourself letting go. But as your brain calms down, reality hits you, and your mentally and emotionally aching for peace once again, back to the horrible truth and fighting the same demons that seem undefeatable. Searching for a way out, but this maze you are trapped in seems like a repeating cycle. You feel as if you came into this world to pay for what you have done in a past life. It feels like you were just born to suffer, and some of us are just luckier than others.

Time for Change

I will not let pain win. I am stronger than the storm,
I will put this hurt in the past, a cold heart turning warm.
I will let my tears run dry. I will rebuild my strength,
I will become a better me and change the way I think.
I will no longer stand stagnate, letting go of the weight I carry,
Ready to jump this hurdle and unleash what was buried.

—I am ready.

Beautiful

People will laugh and judge your mistakes,
forget about the million things that you had done so great.
We go through life wanting to please, but it's
the negative things that everyone sees.
This world can't change unless we change ourselves,
we all have storylike books on a shelf.
People will hurt you and break you down because when one is
unhappy with one's self, they hurt everyone that's around.
People who are unhappy bleed on to those close by.
No need to retaliate, they just hurt on the inside.
Never lose yourself, understand it's OK to hurt,
learn to be happy, and know your worth.

—Every day be a better you.

It's OK to Be You

The world is art, and we are all the definition of beauty.
Don't change who you are to be like the girls in the movies.
Your skin color is beautiful; what you weigh doesn't matter.
Love you for you, you will be much happier.
Live life to the fullest and allow yourself to be great.
Do what makes you happy; don't change because of hate.
Your free to be yourself, to love who you want to love.
People's opinions shouldn't matter; enough is enough.
Who cares about who you vote for, just continue to be kind.
Be OK with opposite opinions, and don't
let the world control your mind.
It's OK to be different; life would be boring if we were the same.
Stop letting others control you and having you live in shame.

—It's OK to be yourself.

Love Is Love

Don't let this world tell you what love looks
like; most of the world is blind,
Hatred within themselves, making them unkind.
Love is many things, mostly actions and not one's words.
Love is a beautiful thing; love should never hurt.
Don't let them tell you what love looks like;
don't compare with internet posts.
Most people post what they want you to see; they do it for the looks.
Be happy with what you have, so long as your healthy and happy.
Don't be like these other girls who just pretend to be.
Love isn't fancy diamonds or a brand-new, fancy car;
love is time and effort; love is from the heart.

—Love is love.

Weighing Me Down

Living with this weight complex has changed me for the worse,
Battling depression, looking at myself hurts.
Can't stand my looks, makeup no longer helps.
Can't even stand on a scale. I hate myself.
I don't see anything beautiful, even the inside turned ugly.
Staring in the mirror, a stranger staring back at me.
Clothes no longer fit me. I leave my hair a mess.
I don't see beauty, I'm stuck, I'm depressed.
They say learn to love yourself, but I have been trying for years.
But nothing changes the ugliness that stairs back into the mirror.
Therapy and pills, it never works; being called beautiful, It still hurts.
I don't love who I am. I can't make peace with myself;
going under the knife is the only thing that helps.

—It's time to make changes.

My Own Battle

I cried today, this time my husband has seen my tears,
Could no longer hold them back, burying this weight complex for years.
I have been pointing my finger for so long, but
it was me who started to change.
Because I hated myself, I thought everyone hated me the same.
If you could see me through my eyes, you would understand,
I try to better myself every day and love myself as much as I can.
But I no longer love myself, and each day, I try to find a reason to,
I let myself go, unsure of what to do.
Even when I wasn't heavy, I still counted my flaws,
fighting every day, trying to tear down these walls.

—Don't let go.

The Wild Child

I was a careless soul, running wild down the rabbit hole.
You couldn't tell me twice, for I was a wild child;
dumb and hardheaded, I was in denial.
I was the kid that parents were warned about, wasn't
allowed to play when the other kids went out.
I didn't like direction. I would swear that I knew it all.
Talking back to teachers, I didn't care at all.
Not sure what was my purpose, just young and dumb,
avoiding situations, every time I would run.
You couldn't put fear in my heart. I thought I was built like a machine,
expelled for fighting anytime kids were mean.
I always learned the hard way; everything
went to one ear and out the other,
until I got older and became a mother.
That's what changed for me and for the better.

—Are children are our heroes.

Post-traumatic Stress

Post-traumatic stress, flashbacks still exist,
Avoiding certain places, places I'll never miss.
Memories I try to bury, somehow float to the surface,
Memories alone can still haunt and hurt us.
The button is stuck on replay. I can't get this to stop,
Trying to avoid this pain, this pain hurts a lot.
I don't want to remember, but life likes to remind me,
Peace within myself, I can't put this behind me.
Trauma from early childhood, I'm followed by the past,
I will carry this for the rest of my life, a sick feeling I can't surpass.
Years have gone by, and I'm begging to forget. Visions
haunt my mind. I need to factory reset.
Every day for me is a struggle. I try my absolute best,
But it keeps catching up, fighting this post-traumatic stress.

—Inhale and exhale.

Almost to the Finish Line

One day you just wake up and you'll feel OK,
your dark demons have gone away.
High off life, weight lifted from your shoulders, sunshine
in your face, it's no longer getting colder.
Positive thoughts, nothing will get in your way,
had waited forever for this brighter day.
You can't erase my smile or take away my laughter. I'm
almost to the stars, my dreams I'm chasing after.
I was always unstoppable, one goal after another. I keep
looking forward, and it continues to get better.
I refuse to fail, even in the dark, I still see. I took chances in
life and kept going when no one else believed in me.
I knew what was best. I was my own best friend, don't
try to judge me until you know where I've been.
I have climbed to the mountaintops, I went swimming with the
sharks, I had guided my own self with monsters in the dark.
You can't take away my kindness, you can't turn my heart cold, I
have survived through battles that would have made anyone fold.
I have cried rivers but still made it across, I had the strength
to make it through when everything else was lost.
I carried bricks on my shoulders with weights strapped to my
feet, you will never change who I am, so please have a seat.
So long I'm still breathing, I will continue to walk with blistered
feet, I'm almost at the finish line with faith when you doubted me.

—Stand strong when doubted.

I Can't Be Fixed

I survived all my life. How do I get out of survival mode?
It's ruining relationships, and it's tearing apart my home.
I see a different person in the mirror, an evil I can't
recognize, the good part of me is buried deep inside.
I need time to myself, to be alone days at a time, to let
go of the madness that keeps following behind.
Not sure how long I will make it, the afterlife sounds more appealing,
I'm beyond capable of being fixed, I'm beyond capable of healing.

—Don't lose your needle and thread.

The Sky Is Dark

The sky is dark, but the rain makes me smile.
Don't want the sunshine for a little while.
I have the devil's grin, I feel alive when it storms,
I'm used to sleeping in a bed full of thorns.
My moods strike like lightning, my voice can rumble like thunder.
My storm is brewing, it's time to take cover.
My moods switch like the seasons, gentle warmth or can be cold.
The weatherman can't guess me, so don't listen to what you are told.
These horns on my head, they fit so perfectly, it's
time for the next season, so let me be.

—It's OK to have alone time.

Let's All Wear the Crown

There's no such thing as white and black,
Like what does that mean?
Separated by race, we are all human beings.
Who cares about your religion, just love from the heart,
Everyone should stick together,
yet we are tearing each other apart.
Who cares about who you love,
we should all be equally free,
This is where we should come together,
I love you and you love me.
Who cares about your political views,
The whole power is built with lies.
Let's all come together,
Show our hearts and let's rise.
Let's all wear the crown of a king and queen,
No one is better than the next,
No such thing as in-between.
Let's put the past behind us,
It's time to lay down our swords,
It's time to open our hearts,
And start wanting to love each other more.

—Don't let the world darken your soul. We are all human.

Put Yourself First

The world stands still when your shoulders are heavy,
Everyone disappears, and your heart becomes heavy.
Where are the ones who were calling you a friend
with all their comments, saying they will be here until the end?
Where are all the friends who said they will have your back,
but when their phone rings, they don't answer or call back?
Where are these so-called friends who claimed to be by your side?
Where are my friends who said they were down to ride?
You see, this is a lesson learned, not everyone in your
corner should call you family, it's earned.
Watch everyone come around when you're no longer in need
and don't ever brag about how you are a friend to me.

—Sometimes you must have your own back first.

Love Yourself in the Dark

I found myself in the darkness, I knew at that moment how strong I was.
Ridiculed by others but it started with self-love.
I envisioned my dreams and started with small goals.
I started loving myself. and I started to grow.
Every time I would fall, I would get up and fight,
it was never easy, deep thoughts, and unable to sleep at night.
Imagine being in a dark room, unable to see and
hear, searching for a door, blind and in fear.
Through all the tears I had not given up, with
one turn, the door opened, I found love.
I found myself, I was happy, nothing could
break my peace or take parts of me.
I became my own best friend and learned to give her what she deserves.
forever washed my hands off the past and put me first.

—Love yourself first and watch the love spread.

Time Is Ticking

Mommy, please love me. I know you're busy.
I just want you to spend some of your time with me.
Don't leave me here alone. I get pretty bored.
No need to spend money if we can't afford.
Just a little time we can draw or play at the park,
Or maybe bedtime stories in the dark.
I just want some of your time,
Right now, it's you I need,
Begging for your attention, come play with me, please.
I'm getting bigger soon. I won't be so small,
I will be all grown up big and tall.
Life is short and time is ticking fast,
Remember, times like this don't last.

—Put the phones and controllers down.

Not Who I Used to Be

I become more of a monster each time I get hurt,
A part of me chipped away when love didn't work.
Pain and betrayal, it changes who you are, left with
scattered pieces, you start taking things too far.
You're unable to trust no matter how much you wanted to.
Everyone will hurt you, that's what your brain teaches you.
I am already ruined, I have worked on myself for years,
I am now hard to love. I live in fear.
I am a monster, my heart cold and black,
The devil has taken over. I can't turn back.

**—You can't take away the memories, but
you can write a new chapter.**

No Destination

I was running away since the age of ten,
but this time, I had run away with a friend.
This time life hit me, I thought I wouldn't live, but
until this day, I'll never forget what he did.
My friend had left me to run off with a guy,
realizing I was alone, I started to cry.
I had walked the dark alleys, left alone in the streets,
but on this night, he took what was left of me.
He pulled me from the alley into an abandoned, run-down
house. I knew this was the end that I would never get out.
No one heard me screaming as I grasped onto the steps.
He dragged me inside, you can guess what happened next.
The thick smell of alcohol lingered on his breath,
Hands around my throat, the other lifting my dress.
I had kicked and screamed, but no one heard my cries,
Just taking the pain with tears running down my eyes.
I felt the weight from his body when laying on top of mine.
I wiped away the tears, telling myself I would be fine.
He walked away into the darkness, my cue to hurry and leave.
Continued walking to nowhere with what was left of me.

—You are not alone.

Chapter 2

THE EXHALE, THE HAPPINESS

Journal

Finally, I breathe, looking back at the years when everything happened. I have finally exhaled. I found myself again. I am so proud of myself because, truth is, I should have never made it. God had a plan for me that I will never fully understand, but it's not meant for me. Here I am, alive and well and blessed to see another day. This journey wasn't easy, but I did it. Of course, I have scars that remain, but that's my mark of strength. Even throughout the greatness, nothing is ever perfect. We must be thankful for what we do have and focus on the here and now. My shoulders feel so much lighter now that I found the light at the end of the tunnel. How did I do it, you ask? Well, it wasn't simple. I just never gave up. It all depends on how bad you want it. Stay humble and know that what was given in life can always be taken away. When you do good things from the heart, good things will follow. Same way vice versa. If you do wrong the bad will follow. Make changes and focus on yourself. Show everyone who said you will never make it, or you will never amount to anything that they were wrong. Your stronger not weak. Life wants you to fail. Keep your circle small and separate yourself from that which no longer gives you peace in life. Your choices have consequences, and it's up to you to make the right ones.

My Littles

I watch you play, and my heart melts, the
most loving feeling I had ever felt.
I brush your hair in the mirror and always call you handsome,
you smile from ear to ear, my heart is never lonesome.
Your little hand in mine, I watch you grow, teaching
you everything possible that there is to know.
I live for my children, they need me the most, my heart
outside my chest, the ones I love the most.
I would give them my last breath, I will fight through any
war, for these two boys, I would do anything for.
They are the reason to keep living, to push when I fall, and
nothing will change even when they grow to be big and tall.
I have two hearts that need me, so I give them mine,
I would do it all over and press rewind.

—We are all they have.

I Never Knew Wishes Would Come True

My life had changed when I met you, you
had pushed me to reach the stars.
You made me feel good again, you're the one that filled my heart.
Relationships are never perfect, but in my eyes, you're perfect to
me, even through the storms, you never stopped loving me.
You loved me when I couldn't love myself, even through the times I
started to change, you never walked away, you still loved me the same.
We will never be perfect or what others expect us to be,
and I love you even more for never giving up on me.
I stand by our vows through rich or poor and sickness and health,
being with you is the most amazing thing I have ever felt.
I wish I had met you sooner, that's the only thing I would have changed,
giving us more chapters in our book, giving us more time for a new page.
You sing a song to my heart, a song I never heard before, you're
different in every way, you're everything I wished for.
You are the love of my life, you are what keeps pushing me
through, my prayers were answered the day I met you.

—I love you.

Heaven's Eyes

Look up to the midnight sky, now what do you see?
Stars that shine so vividly.
They are the eyes that watch over us,
The ones we hold in our hearts.
Our great-grandmother she is,
No one can play that part.
It's OK to feel sad, even at ties, I feel down,
But just because she is not in flesh doesn't mean she is not around.
She has left memories behind,
She has molded a part of you, trust me when
I say she is watching over you.
Look at your success, I know she is smiling from ear to ear.
Prayers do work, even she can hear.
We just learn to adjust because the pain never goes away.
Please continue to smile, we will all meet again someday.
But until then, just look to the skies,
Because she is watching you through what I call heaven's eyes.

—Dedicated to my sister.

And Just Like That

And just like that, my life had changed,
I had awakened one morning, not feeling the same.
My confidence at high and my lows had withered away,
With a smile on my face, my pain had melted away.
And just like that, my prayers were answered,
Healing from the past pain I had encountered.
Even though I have fresh scars, I am smiling within,
Because from this day forward, I refuse to give in.
The air I breathe is different, not so humid and dry,
I can't even count the days the last time I broke down and cried.
I carry my pain differently, using it as lessons instead of weights.
The power is in my hands; what world will I create?
At one point, I was drowning, drowning for such a long time,
Managed to still breathe and pull myself out on time.
And just like that, I'm a survivor, I refuse to lose myself and fall.
Without determination, you will have nothing at all.
I broke free from my prison and fought battles inside my head.
I overcame obstacles and chose happiness instead.
None of us are perfect, keep pushing towards the light.
No matter what happens in life, never ever give up the fight.

—The light will soon shine.

A Promise Was Made

The clouds are dark, and the rain pours heavily.
No sunshine in the skies, sitting here so quietly.
With my feet propped up, hearing the crackling of
the fire, feeling relaxed and not so tired.
Sipping on coffee, away from the crisp air,
Feeling so comfortable, lay back in my chair.
The children are sleeping, finally a moment of rest,
Holding the cross that sits perfectly around my neck.
I say a prayer, thanking him for this new life,
Thanking him for waking me each and every night.
I made him a promise, a promise to never give up,
So I sit back and smile each time I look up.

—Pray.

A Book of Us

My heart opened instantly, an open book for you to read,
You created chapters in my life, writing a future for you and me.
A book of nonfiction, others may call a fairy tale,
No longer holding my breath, you allowed me to exhale.
You became my favorite quote on how love should really be,
A true love story, starting with you and me.
My heart sings a song with every beat inside my chest,
When everyone was the same, you were different from the rest.
Forever writing our story, no such thing as the end,
To be continued forever, sincerely, your best friend.

—Real love doesn't hurt.

Written in the Sand

It's the little things that matter, you make my world a better place,
With your hand in mine and kisses upon my face.
The warmth of your touch, the way your eyes glow with your stare,
The way you hold me at night, sweet gestures that you care.
With your dreams I'm included, you speak our future into existence,
When I need you the most, you're always here to listen.
We have a way with balance, picking up each other's pieces,
Ignoring life around us, we don't care who sees us.
You make life so much easier, my backbone when I am weak,
You're my voice when I'm not heard, during times it's hard to speak.
A life of calmness, like the sound of ocean waves,
The salt upon your lips, I love the way it tastes.
Our bond is inseparable, living in what I call wonderland,
Forever we will be with our names written in the sand.

—Love language.

Overdrive

My body is a machine running in overdrive,
Pushing my limits; because of this, I survived.
No time to slow down, no such thing as a break,
Fulfilling promises to myself that I once made.
Rock bottom is a teacher, giving up is not a choice,
I refuse to settle; you will hear my voice.
I speak high volume, I'm a warrior at its best,
I made it through the dark with daggers in my chest.
My shoulders were heavy, survival is a job,
I can't turn off the switch, I can't make it stop.
My heart protected with thorns, I don't let others pass,
I have been here for myself when no one else has.
"It's time to slow down," I was constantly told,
But who will save me with a hand to hold?
I have been let down by others with promises they can't keep,
I have been let down by most, I'm used to saving myself.
Love is just a word, I need to feel something deeper,
Never running out of fuel, High temperature with survival fever.
I want to give in, to settle with my new life,
But on to the next task, my brain doesn't sleep at night.
What's my next move? Tomorrow I shall see,
Pushing on forward with the machine in me.

—Changes in the making.

I Walk with Him

Standing on the bridge, looking down, I see my past beneath me,
They say the sky is the limit, and I'm shooting
for the stars, and now you see me.
I have miles to go, but this road is no longer lonely,
With GODby my side, he will guide me where I'm meant to be.
I look down at my feet, and my shoes are withered,
I survived through the storms and managed
to stay warm through the blizzard.
I am thankful that god has blessed me with strength and courage.
The path of life isn't easy at times you will get discouraged.
I made a way through the darkest times, but I was never alone.
God had held my hand and walked me home.
My head was held low, but he had lifted my chin,
I constantly prayed and had walked with him.
I wasn't always a believer, but here I am today,
Of course, I once doubted and looked the other way.
He made the sunshine in a way I had never seen,
He opened my eyes to the beauty that was in front of me.
I refuse to be the devil's prey for I am not weak,
I kneel to you, lord, your name I speak.

—Walk with him.

Found My Way

The stars shine brighter than they used to,
I wake with a smile on my face,
Looking up to the sky, I am blessed in many ways.
The air I inhale is much more refreshing,
The mission doesn't stop, constantly progressing.
I see life through different eyes.
Smiles replaced with heavy cries.
It's a feeling like the warm sun hitting your face,
With a small breeze at a steady pace.
I sit back and shoot for the stars,
Making the best out of life and a better tomorrow.

—At the end of the day, you must find your own way.

I Won't Look Back

I dreamt of happiness, and now it's here.
The heaviness is lifted, a smile in the mirror.
My pieces put together, Stronger than I once was,
My heart filled; I thank the man above.
I erased the footprints that lead to my past,
No turning back, walking down a new path.
The sun shines differently, I see life through new eyes,
I thank God every day I survived.

Journal

Married with two kids is the best part of my life.

I am so thankful for what I have now. I prayed and prayed for things to be different. And here I am with my prayers answered. I wanted to change and be a better version of me, and I did. I was given a chance to another day and to create a foundation to build from. Every day, we are all growing; none of us will ever know it all or even have all the answers. We will always have questions and wonder why. Continue to stay humble. What was given can always be taken away. Do things from the heart, and good karma will follow.

Chapter 3

THE VOICES OF OTHERS

A Blessing in a Dark Place

In a time where everything was dark and
lonely, I felt like nothing was right.
I tried to feel, I tried to love, I tried to smile. Nothing worked.
I was stuck, trapped in a house on a hill, a place I hated.
A light came forth.
An older man, a pastor from a long time ago,
Guided me to a place of worship.
I became alive!
For the first time, I felt something I never felt before.
This time I could feel and not be empty.
I can now open my eyes.
I even fell in love with a woman God provided.
I have a lot more than ever in my life. I
turned to God and started praying.
I could not do it alone without him.
I am thankful and loved for the first time.
In this message, I want to reach out to all who are lost and lonely.
Give God a try and let him know you are seeking for answers.
The answers will come in his time. Just don't give up.

Giovanni Cocco

Life without a Rose

Felt like the entire world was on pause. In the year 2020, a pandemic
began called the coronavirus. Nothing around was going right.
Everyone was losing their minds. People were rioting and getting sick.
I felt like I was in a prison, stuck in the house. I was barely getting by
and barely paying off my bills. Work was hard to come by at that time.
I felt heartbroken, and no one to share my
life with. I was alone and felt lost.
I gave up trying to find love and companionship.
I spent a lot of time online, making new friends out of boredom. One
night I received a message from a beautiful woman. Her name was Rose.
She worked as a housekeeper and resided in
Cebu City in the Philippines.
I was a single man for a while, and it felt good to start
something new. She asks more about me and who I was.
I told her bits and pieces as I got to know her.
I was trying to keep a guard up around my heart
after being let down so many times.
A few months went past, and my guard slowly started to
come down. I never felt this way about anyone.
After a while, I was able to meet her son, Zion,
through video chat. He was a little ball of joy.
I told Rose I want to be the dad to Zion and
I wanted to marry her and start a family. I have been waiting
for her country to open back up through this pandemic,
so I can finally meet the woman of my dreams.

It's now May springtime in 2021, and I am still waiting to see
her. I'm patiently waiting to see my future wife and family.
We are still on a lockdown from COVID, but I will not let that
get in my way of us ever meeting. During times like this, it makes
everything hard. It's difficult seeing family, friends, and meeting new
people. This virus has changed the world in many ways, but not for

the better, but I won't allow it to change me. My advice to others is that, go for what you genuinely want. Don't let others get in the way of your happiness. This is your life, not anyone else's. I have dealt with people who looked down on long-distance relationships, but this is my life to live. People will judge but walk on the words of others and make your own dreams come true. I will meet her eventually and will start new beginnings. I learned to be patient that, eventually, good things will come. Always continue to keep your head high.

Giovanni Cocco

My Journal

Hi, everyone. My name is Maurice. I am grateful for so many things in life even though life is hard. I have learned lessons along the way, and it was a rough patch. I guess you could say it was a rough path for me. I have learned to be the bigger person and walked away from problems, such as fights and conflicts. With all of this said, I am thankful for my family and friends. They helped me through a lot, and I'm still going. So we are not alone. It can be a friend or family who can help you and make you happy. Stress, pain, sadness, happiness, love, or anger—we all feel this way, and I am grateful no matter what. Nothing is impossible. Chase your dreams.

Maurice Johnson Jr.
Author's son, age 12

Flight

One day, I want to fly high.
My wings spread so far, so high
And through the sky
I wait for the sun's reply
That if you want to fly
All you need to do is try
It's hard but it's going to be great
I need to make some wings
There's no time to waste
I just have to jump
To start to levitate
I just want to fly
To watch you create
I want to run as fast as I can
And I know that now I have a plan
I can close my eyes and dream
And what I hope is what I've seen
I'll run all the way from land to land
But if you try to just be you,
It will be alright
You can run, have fun, even jump,
But I will take flight.

Josh Colbert

My Story

I'd like to share my story. If it helps one person make a change or difference in their lives, my mission is complete. I'd like to start from the beginning when the depression and anxiety began. I recall being a child around the age of eight years old and feeling so weird and out of place. My stomach would clench, and life was just a bit harder. It stopped for a few years but resurfaced when I was around eleven. I remember it so clearly. The other girls at school played as I sat outside and looked absentmindedly at the sky, worried. I remember, as they teased me about my thighs, the new body I had so recently begun coming into. Let's fast forward to today. There's a lot of trauma and things that could be triggering, including suicide and eating disorder behavior. As I grew up, I was okay. I suffered from my eating disorder for many years off and on, never quite aware that I had one or that it was even a problem. I recall going for a normal doctor's visit, and the discharge papers listed eating disorder as an illness I have. I was thrown off. No doctor had ever mentioned the word "anorexia" to me. The behavior was exacerbated by trauma suffered at the age of fourteen, I've never shared it with many people, and I don't want to go in depth, but it is never your fault. No one has the right to touch or harm your body. This trauma caused me to go into mania. Mania is a part of being bipolar where you get extremely happy and excited and sometimes psychoticand forget what you are doing. It's a mental place you go when you can't handle something. From there, I was diagnosed with bipolar at the age of fourteen. So many pills, so many doctor's appointments. How do you explain to a fourteen-year-old child that they will have a mental illness they have to deal with forever? There is no cure, just keeping symptoms at bay and getting coping skills. Fast forward to age twenty-five. I was in a bad place. My anxiety had become so bad, I thought abusing THC and alcohol would help. I got pregnant with my second child around this time. It was hard, to say the least. I didn't really date his dad for long, and I had no support during my pregnancy. I had never felt more alone in my life. Add to the bipolar part, the pregnancy hormones, and not being able to take my meds I'd been on for years. I became isolated.

I was so worried and nervous about not having my meds. I refused to leave the house. It got so bad, I refused to get out of bed most days, and I begged anyone in my family who could stay to not leave me alone, for fear of suicide and just wanting the feelings to stop. I didn't want to hurt myself or my baby. I simply wanted my brain to rest. Once I had him, it got a lot darker dealing with postpartum depression. However, I'm so happy to say, by the time he was two, I was feeling much better. I was back to myself, and I was ready to get life back on track. So great like someone knew my plans to do better. I suffer from manias in the spring and summer. Well, from summer to fall 2018, I was in a mania where I can't recall most events. I decided, during this time, it'd be smart to have my last child. Well, that happened in September. Let's rewind a bit. I was dating someone off and on, and I got pregnant during an off period. He tried his best to stay around, but I greatly hurt him. Once again I fell straight into a depression this time. It was so bad, the guy I was dating checked on me daily because I wouldn't turn on my phone, and he feared the worse. He's the only person in my life who has ever done that during a depression or even cared if I was okay. He will always, no matter what, hold a deep, special place in my heart. After giving birth to my third son, I again suffered from postpartum. No mother wants to be afraid of life or fearing how to take care of a baby. I'm so happy to say that I got through all that. But here comes anorexia or my eating disorder back with a vengeance. So much so that I starved myself down to the weight I was in high school, and I'm a curvy adult. I never looked at an eating disorder as a mental illness, and many people still don't. This helped me understand a lot, but I thrived from how small I was and, finally, having some control over my life again. The eating disorder has taken me places I'm not proud of. I have treated the ones I love like shit. I had to hit rock bottom where my heart almost stopped because my body was eating that muscle. I got the message inpatient and worked my way through the program. I'm not ashamed to say I've been inpatient, outpatient, and intensive outpatient back and forth, the last time being in March. This disease is the number 1 mental illness with the outcome, death. It is not something I am proud of or would want. It is something I realized during the depths of my pain. I used it as a coping mechanism not to feel when I couldn't handle reality. Yes, I struggle still. Some days, my anxiety is so bad, I want to self-talk myself out of work or eating or things most people who can function have no problems with. I'm not aware of the damage I have truly caused my body; however, with treatment, I can be healthy emotionally. I can share my voice and opinions. I can set boundaries I never knew were needed. I am thriving, and many people would look at me and say, "How?" You are suffering daily. Well, you know what, my suffering has made me a positive, happy, grateful person for the good days and for my kids, for the happiness and beauty the world offers.

I may have bipolar, but I also have a beautiful mind. Never give up. I am a single mom of three beautiful boys. I am working and living my passion. I can support us, and I can cope daily, so my issues don't affect them. Mental illness is not the end. Addiction isn't the end. Everything can change for the better. I look at my semi-colon tattoo on my arm as a reminder each day that I am strong, and I didn't give up. I paused and worked through them. I am not my illnesses. I am a beautiful black woman who is flourishing after being held down for so long by so many adversities.

Danielle Jones

Survival from Abuse

Hi, I'm twenty-four and my name is London. I moved to Vegas, and I met someone online through Facebook when I was twenty-three and she was thirty-three. She also lived in Vegas. We texted and called each other every day and night. One day, we decided to meet in person. She was the sweetest and funniest person I ever met. We had so much in common, I could have never guessed she was the person that put scars on my face, body, and mind.

I stayed with her at her house for a couple of weeks. We moved pretty fast. We got married. "What happens in Vegas stays in Vegas" is what they say, but we had our arguments. We started to not see eye to eye, but I didn't think anything about it. I blamed IVF, which is something women get when they want to get pregnant. She wanted twins, so she was going through mood swings, but after a couple of months, we ended the relationship. We moved on in life. After a couple of months, we got back together. (She was no longer on IVF.)

I moved to Hawaii with her. That's when the nightmare happened. It started with belittling me, and the arguments every day again. She would get mad at me for the smallest things. Don't get me wrong, we did have our good days and we have fun. I was deeply in love with her. The first time she hit me, I threatened to leave, and I got a busted lip for it. The second time she hit me was during an argument, which also led to her hands on my neck. She threatened to stab me like she did her ex, she said. I thought I was going to die that night. The next day, I woke up and had bruises on my arms and felt the soreness on my back, and the back of my head was extremely sore. My throat was so swollen, it hurt to breathe and smile. I ended up with a black eye when I told her I was going to leave. The third time messed up the toilet, and she locked me out of the house, but because I was banging on the door and neighbors came out, she said I was trying to embarrass her. As I was walking in, she grabbed me from behind, hitting me, and knocked me on the ground, aiming to punch my face and trying to move my arms away from my face. After that, I just stayed on the ground, curled up in a ball, crying, thinking every beating I got was my fault. If I did things differently, she wouldn't have gotten mad and put her hands on me. That day, she was acting nice to me again, which was normal. She would be nice and talk to me like she never put her hands on me, or she would go out to buy me some food or ice cream, etc. But that same day I contacted close friends to tell them that if anything happened to me, that I love them and was sorry for anything I've done and not staying in contact. I thought one day this woman was really going to kill me, but I loved her, and I didn't want to leave. I would do anything for her to try and make her happy. But my friends got me a plane ticket to leave. I left with nothing but my phone and the clothes on my back. I was going to turn back around and stay, but I didn't, and I left. She called and texted me, telling me how much she loved me, and she said it won't happen again. I cried on the whole plane ride because I didn't want to leave. But here I am now, free! I am now back in Maryland. I have my own place, a new job, and was promoted. I was finally able to let go. Remember, if it happens once, it will happen again. Just leave because it will never stop. If anyone loves you, they wouldn't put their hands on you. Always remember it's not your fault. I am a lesbian who is a survivor of physical and mental abuse by another woman.

London Brooks

My Baby Was Born

I grew up with multiple health problems. Over the years, I had miscarriage after miscarriage. The doctors told me I would not be able to have any children. Little did they know, years later, a miracle happened. I started having really bad stomach pains the same day I saw my godfather in the hospital for the last time before they pulled the plug. I went to a different hospital to find out I was three months pregnant, but in my mind, I had so many miscarriages, I just knew I was going to lose my baby. I was never able to have a connection with him while I carried him. I had extra fluid around my baby, protein in my urine, and my pressure was extremely high. I had to stay in the hospital for three consecutive months and had twenty-four-hour monitoring because of the risks on my health and because of my history of miscarriages. Even through all the waiting and with the care from the nurses and staff, I had my baby. From that day forward, my life had changed. I became a better me. My son was premature, weighing 3 lb. and 3 oz. He stayed in the NICU for four weeks then was transported to Mount Washington Pediatric Center for continued care. I stayed there for six months. I had a little bit of health problems, but I was able to bring my baby boy home. I was finally able to exhale. It was hard for me, going through all of that. I was emotionally, mentally, and physically drained. I can't believe, to this day, I am finally a mother. This is the biggest blessing I had ever received. The doctor told me I would never be able to have kids, but God had a different plan for me.

Latia Davis

Phoenix

I suppose I should write something that's empowering right now, but my heart won't let me.

Too often I am the phoenix, but now maybe I'm just a butterfly.

Feeling the pain all the time is inevitable, but healing takes courage.

Stepping out of comfort and into a foreign territory is courage.

I want to be this woman that is so strong and so fierce.

Yet here I am on the inside of my soul, as sensitive and gentle as humanly possible.

I cry on the kitchen floor.

It's been too many cold nights that my tears have fallen on this floor in defeat.

But I always rise up to the challenge of standing up after I fall.

And I tell the universe that it hits like a bitch!

Knock me down again if you can! Harder this time!

I stand, flap my wings at my tears, and smile.

I'm still fiery.

I'm still here.

But tonight is different.

I stay down . . .

I cut my wings off and drown in myself.

Guts out on the floor.

Wingless and Gutless.

Why am I drowning?

Why am I watching silently as I destroy myself?

I can't sleep.

I can't eat.

She's on a mission of self-destruction.

And all I can do is watch until she's ready to stop.

Please stop!

STOP!

I take a knife to my wrist and hesitate. . .

I have to stop.

. . .

This metamorphosis has taken me years upon years to complete.
Am I the butterfly?
Or am I the phoenix?
Am I delicate and praying for better days?
Or am I rough and know I can conquer everything.
Or am I both?
Am I sad yet happy?
Am I strong yet have these weaknesses?
Am I hurt but healing?
Oh, is this the part where I tell you how to heal?
I can't tell you that.
Wipe your tears and rise is all I can say.
Whether you are the phoenix or butterfly,
Start again.
Find a way to change, to morph, to adapt, to love again, to feel again.
To be both again.

Brianna Bera

Unforgiven

Who would've known?
Years of knowing someone and they turn out to be the very reason for the nights you stay awake questioning it all.
Questioning your self-worth.
Crying until your chest aches.
Wishing somebody would come to take the very air from your lungs, so you can stop breathing.
And still so much emotion at the very thought of it to this day.
All because of one person
Who chose to hurt me,
Who chose to lie to me,
Who chose to break me.
God, I wish I could take it all back.
The fake forgiveness I gave you . . .
So others could stop questioning and asking when I'd get over it.
You do not deserve my forgiveness.
You took my body and destroyed my mentality all at once.
You had no right.
NONE!
We are told as victims to forgive the ones that have stabbed us, raped us, and attempted to murder our very existence.
Forgive . . . so that WE may move on?
But why?
What if my way of healing is telling you that you don't deserve my forgiveness?
Forgiveness to me means that it was okay to steal a piece of me.
That it was okay to destroy my soul.
That it was okay to watch me disappear mentally for years.
NO! I refuse.
I'm taking my power back!
Taking my forgiveness back.
You are NOT forgiven.

I am worth more than forgiving someone who isn't sorry.
I am worth more to myself than forgiving someone who doesn't see any
wrong in their actions.
You watched me crumble,
You watched me suffer,
You made a fool of me.
You won.
But now . . .
It's my turn!
I will not tell you what you want to hear.
I will not give you so much as a credit for my healing by any means.
You can burn for all I care.
You laid hands on my bare soul.
And took what you wanted and threw me out like trash.
I still remember the anger in your eyes. The gleam of rage
Etched into my brain for eternity.
You will not tell me how to heal or tell me to forgive.
You are unworthy of my energy.
Written all over my face was pain once upon a time.
I wore it like a tattoo of shame and dishonor.
Now . . .
I will look you in the eyes
Head held high
And not feel a damn thing . . .
And that . . .
Is more powerful than you could ever be.

Brianna Bera

Pain changed me, but I survived, and now I am free.

We are not alone.